Community Helpers

Farmers

by Dee Ready

Reading Consultants:
Alice Gudex and William Gudex
Members of the U.S. Farmers Association

Bridgestone Books
an Imprint of Capstone Press

Bridgestone Books are published by Capstone Press
818 North Willow Street, Mankato, Minnesota 56001
Copyright © 1997 by Capstone Press
Printed in the United States of America

Library of Congress Cataloging-in-Publication Data
Ready, Delores.
    Farmers/by Dee Ready
    p. cm.--(Community helpers)
    Includes bibliographical references and index.
    Summary: Explains the clothing, tools, schooling, and work of farmers.
    ISBN 1-56065-511-9
    1. Farmers--Juvenile literature. [1. Farmers. 2. Occupations.]
    I. Title. II. Series: Community Helpers (Mankato, Minn.)
HD8039.F3R4   1997
630' .203'73--dc21

                                        96-48320
                                          CIP
                                           AC

Photo credits
Unicorn/Joel Dexter, cover; Aneal Vohra, 8, 10; Jean Higgins, 16
FPG/Arthur Tilley, 4; Steve Hix, 6; Steven Gottlieb, 12; Frank Cezus, 14;
  Dick Luria, 18; John Lawlor, 20

Table of Contents

Farmers

Farmers work many hours so that people will have food. Some farmers grow crops of fruits, vegetables, and grains. Other farmers raise livestock such as cows, pigs, and chickens.

What Farmers Do

Some farmers plow the ground and plant seeds. Crops grow from the seeds. Other farmers raise cows and sell the milk and meat. Some farmers grow fruits.

What Farmers Wear

Farmers work hard and get dirty. Many farmers wear overalls or jeans. They wear boots in the barnyard. Farmers often wear baseball caps to shade their eyes.

Tools Farmers Use

Farmers use many different tools. Crop farmers use machinery to plant and harvest crops. Dairy farmers use machines to milk their cows. All farmers use small tools such as shovels and rakes.

What Farmers Drive

Farmers drive tractors. A tractor pulls a plow to break up the ground. A tractor also pulls a planter to plant seeds. At harvest time, a combine collects the grain in a bin.

Farmers and School

Farmers need to know how to use their land well. Many farmers study at agricultural college. They study plants and animals. They learn how to make money from their farm work.

Where Farmers Work

Farmers often live on the farm where they work. They usually live in a farmhouse with their families. Farms can be small or large. Most farms have barns, silos, and fields.

People Who Help Farmers

Livestock farmers need veterinarians. A vet helps keep the farmer's animals healthy. Farmers depend on business people. The business people buy the crops or animals and sell them.

Farmers Help Others

Without farmers, there would not be any food. Farmers grow a lot of the food that people eat. Farmers do not just help the people in their own communities. They help people all around the world.

Hands On: Plant and Grow Beans

Farmers grow food for everyone in the world. You can grow crops, too. All you need are seeds, soil, water, and sunshine.

1. Fill paper cups about half full with dark, moist soil.
2. Use your finger to make a hole. Put the hole in the center of the soil in each cup.
3. Plant one bean seed in each of the holes.
4. Cover the seeds with soil. Sprinkle the soil with water.
5. Put the cups where they will get plenty of sun. Water your seeds a little each day.

Words to Know

combine (KAHM-bine)—a machine that cuts plant stalks and then separates the grain

community (kuh-MEW-nuh-tee)—a group of people who live in the same area

crop (KRAHP)—a plant grown to feed animals or to sell for food

dairy farmer (DAIR-ee FAR-mur)—someone who raises cows, milks them, and sells the milk

harvest (HAR-vist)—to gather a crop

livestock (LIVE-stahk)—animals raised on a farm to milk or sell for food

silo (SYE-loh)—a tall, round building used to store food for animals

Read More

Brady, Peter. *Tractors*. Mankato, Minn: Bridgestone Books, 1996.

Gibbons, Gail. *Farming*. New York: Holiday House, 1988.

Knightley, Rosalinda. *The Farmer*. New York: Macmillan, 1987.

Kunhardt, Edith. *I Want to Be a Farmer*. New York: Grosset & Dunlap, 1989.

Internet Sites

Future Farmers of America

http://www.ffa.org/

I & J Farms of Idaho

http://cyberhighway.net/~ijfarms/index.htm

Index